JEFFREY'S STORY
A TIME OF SICKLE CELL CRISIS
WRITTEN BY ANGEL CILLY CELL
ILLUSTRATED BY LAURIE DEKATCH
SUPER CILLY CELL CHARACTER DESIGNED BY CALEB JOHN WOODS

MISS NELSON
4th GRADE
Today's Lesson:
EMPATHY

"Miss Nelson!
It is two o'clock and
time for recess,"
said Jeffrey excitedly.

"Settle down Jeffrey,
we are going right now,"
Miss Nelson replied.
She knew he had been
waiting for recess ALL day.

Jeffrey, Suzie and Paris always have fun playing jump rope at recess. It is one of Jeffrey's FAVORITE games.

"Suzie, I am starting to feel **VERY TIRED**. I need to sit down and rest for a while," said Jeffrey.

Suzie sighed. "Don't you want to practice for field day? I'm hoping to get first place this year. Jeffrey, are you feeling okay?"

"I don't mean to let you down, I want to win, too," said Jeffrey, "but I'm in a lot of **PAIN** right now. Can you please get Miss Nelson for me?"

Paris and Suzie _ran_ to get Miss Nelson.

"Miss Nelson! Miss Nelson! Jeffrey is crying!" they shouted.

"Calm down girls... so you can tell me what happened," said Miss Nelson.

"He said he is **HURTING** very badly and he needs your **HELP!**" they replied.

"Jeffrey, what's wrong? Is it your *Sickle Cell?*" asked Miss Nelson.

"I think so. Can you please help me? The **pain** is unbearable," cried Jeffrey.

"Certainly Jeffrey," assured Miss Nelson, "I will take you to the nurse's office so she can give you some **MEDICINE** while we wait for the ambulance. I will also call your dad to let him know what has happened."

"Just keep being **STRONG** and I know you will make it through this," encouraged Miss Nelson.

"Excuse me nurse... I am here for my son,
Jeffrey Pass, how is he doing?" asked Jeffrey's father.

"Hello Mr. Pass, Jeffrey is doing much better, he is
finally resting," said Nurse Sheppard. "He is a sweet kid,
we don't like it when he goes into SICKLE CELL CRISIS."

"Me too, this is his third time in two months. It makes
me feel pretty helpless at times," he shared. "This
disease is a lot for a child to bear, but I know he will
get through it... he is a fighter. Jeffrey says I am his
HERO, but he is the one that inspires me."

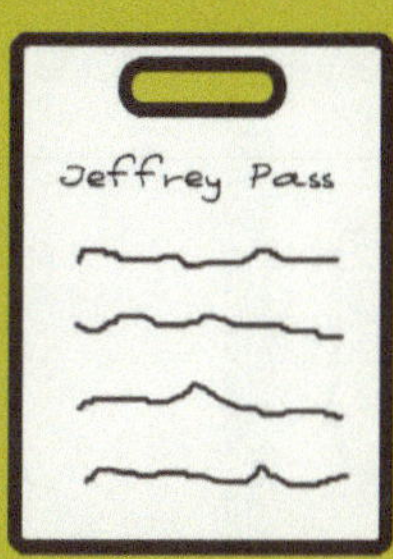
Jeffrey Pass

"Dad! Dad!"

"How's my boy?" asked Mr. Pass.

"I'm doing good now, dad. Can I go home?" replied Jeffrey.

"Are you just saying that because you don't want to be admitted to the HOSPITAL?" asked his father.

"No dad, I really do feel better." answered Jeffrey. "I'm sorry you had to leave work early, I don't know what happened... all of a sudden I was in a lot of pain."

"Son, son... it is okay. Please DO NOT WORRY about all of that now. You just need to rest. I am here for you & GOD always makes a way for us." said Mr. Pass.

"Well hello there young man, how are you feeling?" asked Dr. Freemon.

"Much better, thank you," said Jeffrey.

Dr. Freemon continued, "Your lab results weren't too bad, but you were a little **dehydrated**, which is probably what started your pain crisis."

"Well I think I can manage my pain at home now," said Jeffrey.

"Okay Jeffrey, we will give you another bag of **FLUIDS** and if you still feel you can manage it at home, I will give you some medicine to help you once you leave here," said the doctor. "You will also have to stay out of school tomorrow, you will need to get some good rest. Your nurse will be right in to make sure your pain is under control, and **hopefully** our next visit will be in my office. Take care you two."

"Thanks Dr. Freemon," said Mr. Pass.

"Later Doc!" said Jeffrey.

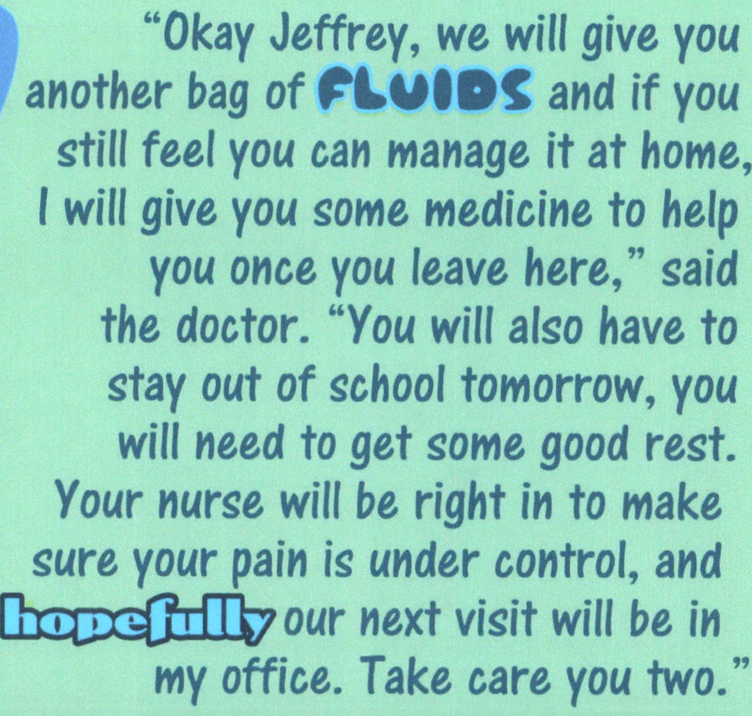

Facts about:
SICKLE CELL
DISEASE
"SIK-ULSELL DIS-EESE!"

"Miss Nelson, I am really concerned about Jeffrey! Why has he not been here? Why does he start to hurt all of a sudden?" asked Suzie.

"Is he okay? Is it his *Sickle Cell*?" asked Paris.

"I figured you guys would have a lot of QUESTIONS so I invited a friend of mine who is going to share some information that will help you understand what Jeffrey is going through," replied Miss Nelson.

"Now I would like to introduce you to SUPER CILLY CELL! Tell CILLY 'Hi' boys and girls," said Miss Nelson.

"Hi CILLY!" screamed the children.

"Hi everyone. I'm SUPER CILLY CELL and I am here to talk to you about *SICKLE CELL DISEASE*. Children, can you say *SIK-ULSELL DIS-EESE*?"

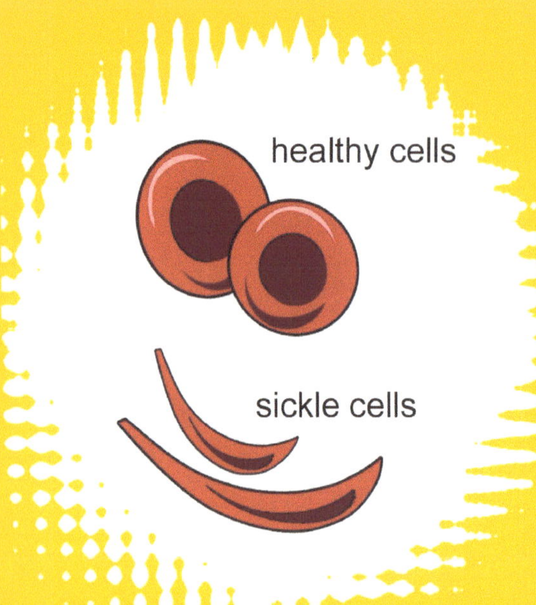

SICKLE CELL DISEASE

is a disease of the blood.
It gets its name because a person's
red blood cells are shaped like sickles or
crescent moons, instead of their usual
round, disc shape.

When red blood cells are shaped like sickles
they can get stuck inside blood vessels. This keeps
blood from FLOWING properly in the body, which can
cause a lot of pain. Important organs like the brain, heart
and kidneys need constant blood flow to work correctly.

People who have *Sickle Cell* may feel pain when
their blood vessels get clogged with sickle cells.
The pain can last a few minutes or several days.
It might hurt a lot or just a little. When this
happens, it is called a SICKLE CELL CRISIS
(a CRISIS means a time of trouble).

No one knows when sickle cells might get stuck and *CLOG* a blood vessel. Certain conditions, like if a person gets cold, sick or doesn't drink enough fluids, can lead to a **SICKLE CELL CRISIS.** Doctors and nurses can help by giving them medicine and getting them rehydrated.

Because people with *Sickle Cell* do not have enough normal blood cells, they may get tired more easily and might even get sick more often. *GOOD REST* and a HEALTHY DIET are NECESSARY.

It is important to have a nutritious diet with PLENTY of fruits, vegetables (especially green leafy vegetables) and LOTS and LOTS of **WATER.** Fluids are number one in importance. People with *Sickle Cell* should drink as much water as possible each day to prevent dehydration.

" **SUPER CILLY CELL**, can we catch *Sickle Cell* like Jeffrey and become sick or in pain?" asked Suzie.

"Sickle Cell Disease is INHERITED. Say, 'IN-HAIR-UH-TED'?"

The children repeated, "IN-HAIR-UH-TED."

"That means you can't catch it like you can a cold or the flu. Children are born with the disease when both parents pass along the *sickle cell disease gene* to their children," answered CILLY. "The disease affects many different races, and every person with *Sickle Cell* is affected differently."

"Well I HOPE that I have answered all your questions today, boys and girls. But before I go, I have SOMEONE here I think you might want to see..." said CILLY.

"It's Jeffreyyy!!!" the children shouted.
"Hi Jeffrey, we MISSED YOU! Are you okay?"

"I AM FEELING MUCH BETTER. THANKS EVERYBODY!"
smiled Jeffrey.

ANGEL CILLY CELL
TOTALLYHEALEDNETWORK.ORG

The author and creator of The Cilly Cell Project was given an incredible vision after being diagnosed with Hemoglobin SC, a type of sickle cell disease. Fighting through the pain and grief of a chronic illness, she foresaw a way to provide hope to others that were facing the same battle. Angel's goal is to use the Cilly Cell character as a mascot that can visit children in hospitals during their sickle cell crisis, as well as bringing Cilly into schools to help foster awareness and empathy to those enduring this life-long disease.

"I want to see the light of hope in every life we help, see them living healthy, whole lives and totally healed by the blood of Jesus!"

- Angel Cilly Cell

LAURIE DEKATCH

Laurie is an illustrator with a divine purpose to help inspire, educate and heal families during difficult times of illness, disease and stress by opening up avenues of communication through the art of illustrating and storytelling.

"Be always with a gracious heart and all will be possible."

- Laurie DeKatch

Your Donations Will Help Us Provide...

...for a child who comes to the hospital in **Sickle Cell Crisis** to get a visit from **Cilly** and leave with a kit that has a water bottle, a copy of this book, as well as a miniature stuffed **Cilly Cell** doll.

• • • Your donations will also help us to aid families to cover bills and other expenses that occur because of this disease. A child with **Sickle Cell** can visit the hospital up to 18 times in a year. That can put an extreme amount of financial hardship on the family. • • •

TWITTER
@ANGELCILLYCELL

Angel Cilly Cell

TOTALLYHEALEDNETWORK.ORG

404)491-9505

THE CILLY CELL PROJECT/

ANGEL CILLY CELL
-FOUNDER-